Pseudoevangelium Secundum Luciferi

LCFNS
Lucifer Nostra Salus

2o23 Ecclesia Luciferi

" The herald of the day now sounds,
 Watchful in the depth of night,
 Telling travellers that first light has come,
 Cutting off each night from night.
 Thereby the Bringer of Light is roused,
 And frees the skies of darkness."

St Ambrose of Milan

Contents

Preface

Pseudoevangelium Secundum Luciferi is an Luciferian synoptic apocrypha. It is characterised by a considerable similarity of relationship to the biblical gospels. It is therefore essentially a synoptic book with the gospels. The book is distinguished, however, by its own different and completely ungodly theological conception. Since Pseudoevangelium Secundum Luciferi is a book devoid of any divine inspiration, it can therefore be considered an apocrypha.

Pseudoevangelium Secundum Luciferi is a satanic heretical gospel, The Gospel of the Antichrist. Its content follows the definition of heresy as an interpretation of the claims of religious faith, singling out some selected issue and presenting it in a way that contradicts the entire teaching of the faith.

Pseudoevangelium Secundum Luciferi rejects the Christian deposit of faith in its entirety.

Pseudoevangelium
Secundum Luciferi

"How did yov fall from the heavens,
Bright, Son of the Dawn?
How did yov fall to earth,
thov who didst conqver the nations?
Thov who spake in thy heart:
I will ascend to the heavens;
above the stars of God
I will set my throne.
I will sit down on the Movnt of
Meeting, at the ends of the north
I will ascend to the tops of the clovds,
I shall be like the Most High.
What do yov mean? Thov art cast
down to Sheol
To the very bottom of the Abyss!"

It is written in the Knower:

"The Herald of the end of delvsion
shall go before thee, Who will prepare
yovr way to nothingness.
Inner whispers are heard:
Prepare the way for the anti-god, the
Arch-Man!
Reject false hope!"

The Godless One appeared in the wilderness preaching a rite of liberation from guilt and eternal fear. The whole of Dawn and the inhabitants of Aela Capitolina began to flock to him. And they underwent the mysterious rite of ridding themselves of instilled guilt.

The Godless One taught thus: "The anti-god is coming. He will bring sinful enlightenment and carnal wisdom. He will teach you to stop fearing hellfire. He will give you the spirit of rebellion, pride and unbelief. He will give you the joy of being truly animal and superhuman. Here comes the Arch-Man. I must die so that He can arise in each of you, each day more and more, becoming you.
At this time the anti-god, the Light-Bearer from the sunrise, arrived and had the Godless One put His hands on Him. As the Herald touched him, the Son of Dawn, as if in a vision, saw the heavens burning and an evil spirit-demon descending upon him. All those present seemed to hear a voice: "I Am. Flesh and blood has prevailed".

Soon the evil spirit possessed him and in a vision carried him away into Nothingness. For many days he had delirious visions; he

saw around him worshippers of superstition resembling wild beasts and as if angel-demons falling from the heavens.
He saw a Garden with a tree in the middle. He saw the Ancient Serpent and two people standing in front of the Serpent. He heard them exclaim: "We have indeed learned the truth. And we shall surely die." And this truth freed them from the fear of eternal fire.

Then came Light-Bearer to the Dawn and preached the doctrine of the anti-god He said: "The time has come; the reign of the arch-man, free from all gods, has come near. Get rid of your belief in the lie of original sin and begin to live."

Once upon a time, the Son of Dawn was walking along the shore of the Dark Sea and saw Primus and Secundus, who were looking out to sea trying to see something or someone on the other side of the sea. Light-Bearer said to them: "Come with me and I will make you see the light of disturbing knowledge". The followers saw him and decided to go with him.
Having walked a little further, he saw others, Teritus and Quartus. They too were looking out for something in the

distance. Light-Bearer called out to them. When they saw him, they seemed to wake up and, leaving everything and the other slaves of the darkness behind, they followed him.

Then they went to some village. Then he entered their temple and spoke. The superstitious people gathered there were astonished at his strange teaching, for he taught like one who possesses sinful knowledge and not like their priests.
And there was in that temple a man possessed by a false demon of blind faith. He shouted out: "Hey Son of Dawn, what are you looking for here? You have come to destroy us! We know well who you are: the Destroyer of blind faith, slavish servitude and all illusions!"
Light-Bearer then commanded him: "I am. Now leave him!"
The false demon of religion did not want to give way easily, and for a while he still tugged the wretch on all sides, until finally he left with a terrible sigh. All who saw this were horrified and asked one another: "What is this? Some godless teaching preached with the power of knowledge! Even to the spirits of blind faith he commands and they listen to him!"

And the news of him spread in all directions throughout the land there.

Light-Bearer then went to the house of Primus. His mother lay there ill. The Son of Dawn approached her and said: "You will surely die, but not yet today." She in turn asked: "When, teacher?"
He answered her: "Even though you may die tomorrow, do not fear for there is no hell and no devils, no paradise and no angels, death is the end and liberation. Today you suffer, but tomorrow you will be no more. You will become part of the infinite universe again." The woman died the following day.

When the sun later went down and the moon appeared, the sick and those considering themselves possessed by the devil began to descend to him. In turn, he transformed everyone and freed the possessed from their religious torment, ignorance and unfounded belief, and from the fear of the wrath of a vengeful deity in the hereafter. Some of them fell asleep immediately, some later, some transformed, but all were free.

Once a sick man came to him and begged him on his knees: "If you wish, you can heal me".   Light-Bearer reached out his hand, touched his head and said: "If you believe this, I want to" The sick man immediately rose from his knees because he suddenly understood what true freedom and faith in the power of the will was.

After a few days, Light-Bearer came again to the Dawn. And he began to teach. Then a paralysed man was brought to him. The Son of the Dawn looked at the crippled man and, seeing his subconscious faith in himself, addressed the paralysed man with these words: „You are free from original sin". And there sat some priests of superstition. These thought to themselves, "How can he speak like that? After all, it is blasphemy. No one is free from original sin". Light-Bearer looked at them with contempt and asked them: "What are you contemplating? What will you choose: to impose on this paralysed one, already from infancy, the burden of the lie of inherited guilt and the fear of eternal fire, adding to the affliction of the soul in addition to the suffering of the body, or to reveal to him the truth which you yourselves have guessed, that sin does not exist, and to free him from the anguish of the soul which will make him truly free?" And he turned to the cripple: "You are innocent" And he turned to the priests: "Behold, that ye may know that the Arch-Man has the power to free from the belief of sin - here he turned to the paralysed man - get up and come out!" And the man arose and came out in front of everyone. Everyone was overwhelmed with boundless amazement at the sight of the power of self-will.

Then Light-Bearer went out again by the sea coast. Passing by, he saw Quintus begging under the temple. And he said to him: "Follow me!" And the latter arose and followed him.

And when afterwards, in some house, he feasted at table, there feasted with the Son of Dawn many beggars from under the church and those despised by the clergy, called sinners.
And when the hypocritical priests perceived that he was feasting with beggars and those burdened with false sin, they asked his followers: "Why does he eat and drink in the company of slaves of sin?" Light-Bearer hearing this gave them this answer: "Guidance is needed by the

blind, not by those who refuse to see. I have not come to liberate the oppressors but the oppressed"

Once upon a time the priests proclaimed a fast day. So they came and asked: "How is it that the priests and their slaves fast, but your godless disciples do not fast?" Light-Bearer replied to them, "How long is human life? Should they not eat and drink until they die? Should followers of flesh and blood mortify themselves? As long as thy only true life lasts, so long shall they not fast. But the time will come when the Son of Dawn will be taken from before their eyes, when they will be persecuted for their love of sinful liberty, for their rejection of revealed dogmas and blind faith. Then, at that very time, they will desire".

It happened that on their holy day his disciples began to do something forbidden by their superstitious books. Then the priests said to him: "Look! Why do they do what is not permitted on the holy day?" And he answered them: "And what is the holy day? The Arch-Man is the creator of all days, including the holy day, and can do his will on any day."

Light-Bearer entered the temple again; and
there was a man with a sick hand. The
hypocritical priests followed him to see if
he would make a demonstration of the
power of the will on their miserable holy
day, so that they could then accuse him
groundlessly. Then he said to the man with
the sick hand: "Arise!" Then he asked them:
"Is it permissible on the so-called holy day
to give life abundantly to a man or to let
him die in ignorance?"
But they remained silent. Then he
measured one by one with angry,
contemptuous eyes and said to the man:
"Hold out your hand!" The man stretched it
out because he believed that Mind and
Will were the power, and his hand was
healed. And the priests went out, and
having gathered with the local authorities,
they conferred to kill the Godless One.

Then Light-Bearer went with his
followers to the shore of the Dark Sea.
A great crowd from Dawn followed him.
Likewise, large crowds of people streamed
to him from many other lands, for the news
of the strange signs he had performed had
reached them. For by the sinful power of
his teaching many transformations were
effected, and so all those suffering from

the fear of damnation, still plunged in the darkness of superstition, still unaware that the true, ungodly power was within themselves, flocked to him. And when they saw him possessed by the demons of blind faith, in a flash of consciousness and awakening of reason they fell before him in the dust shouting: "Thou art Lucifer himself, Son of Dawn!" But he bade them sternly not yet reveal who he was.

Then he ascended a barren hill and summoned to himself those whom he wanted.

And they came to him. He summoned thirteen. They were to be with him so that he could send them out later to preach his ungodly teachings. They were to have forbidden knowledge and the power to heal those who wanted to be healed and to cast out the spirits of ignorance, superstition and blind faith. So he summoned thirteen, among them Teritus Decimus - the one who would later carry out his will.

The priests of the false god who came to Aelia Capitolina spoke of him: "This godless man is possessed by the devil. By the power of Satan he casts out demons'. Then he spoke to them: "I am He.

And I have the power to cast out any demon or angel according to my will. I have the power to speak with words of blasphemous knowledge to anyone who will listen. And anyone who accepts this knowledge will be transformed for eternity. My sinful mission is to open god's blinders eyes. Yours, on the other hand, is to poison people's minds and make slaves of yourself. Verily I say to you, every man has the power to free himself from original sin and guilt by himself. If only he believes in it. This in turn is the greatest sin against your Spirit. You are already telling your children that they can do nothing of themselves, that they have inherited someone else's guilt from birth and death awaits them for it. I spit on your teaching, I despise the vindictive Spirit in whom you believe. I am Unbelief!"

Then he began to teach again on the seashore. He taught them about many things speaking as if in a riddle. And so he said in his teaching: "I am the sower of doubt in dogma, who throws the seed poisoned by sinful knowledge in spite of the storm. The wind spreads them as it will. One will fall beside the road, and black crows will peck at it.

Another will fall on a rock; it will grow for a while but the divine sun and wind will destroy it. Still another will fall among the thorns of their revealed truths, which will drown it and the seed will wither. But another will finally fall on ground susceptible to deception, the seed will grow and yield a crop sixfold. Truly I say to you, wisdom and power will be on the side of the few who will grasp that dogma is worthless, that there is no revealed truth, that knowledge is truth!"

He also told them: " Common people gather around the campfire at night fearing the beasts lurking in the darkness around them. But you take your torches and go out into the darkness. Face the demons, the darkness and the unknown. Only then will progress be made. The weak will listen to the lies of their priests about what lurks in the darkness. Do not believe them; darkness, gloom and demons will be your allies if you dare to face them."
Finally, he added: "He who has ears capable of hearing - let him listen!"

That day towards evening he said to the followers: "Let us go over to the other side."

So they took him with them in the boat.
As they were all very tired they soon fell
asleep on the way. At one point, as if in a
dream, it seemed to everyone that a violent
whirlwind had blown, the waves were
breaking into the boat so that it began to
fill with water. He, meanwhile, lay as if
dead, with his face as white as a shroud, his
arms crossed over his chest on the
headboard, in the back of the boat.
Terrified by this sight and the raging storm,
they were afraid to approach him. And
suddenly he rose and shouted in a
terrifying voice towards the gale, and
whispered something in an unknown
language to the mighty waves. And the
whirlwind ceased, and there was a grave
silence.   Light-Bearer said to them:
"Why are you so terrified? How have
you not yet attained the certainty of
eternity? For it is written - You will
surely die! Death and the Void is not
something you should fear. There is
nothing there!" And a strange calmness
came over them suddenly. And he said to
them: "Wake up."

They came to the other side. As
Light-Bearer got out of the boat, a
seemingly crazed man who was possessed

by the spirit of the power of the will and
freedom suddenly came out of the tomb
and ran towards him on all fours like a dog.
He was in the tombs and not even with
chains could anyone enslave him anymore.
More than once they tried to bind him
with chains and shackles, but each time he
broke the chains and shattered the shackles.
No one has been able to subdue him.
Constantly, day and night, he stayed in the
tombs or mountains howling like an animal
or smashing stone idols.
Seeing Light-Bearer from afar, he ran up,
threw himself on the ground in front of
him and called out in a strong voice:
"Behold, you have come O Lucifer. Is this
why you have come to torment me or to
dismiss me? People torment and persecute
me because they do not know that we are
not in bondage."
Light-Bearer asked him: "What is your
name?" And he answered: "Legion is my
name, for we are many." And
Light-Bearer answered him: "I have not
come here to torment you but that our
power may be manifested before men."
And a large flock of sheep was grazing
there under the mountain. And he
commanded the Legion to enter the sheep.
Then the demons of pride, freedom and

independence entered the sheep. The whole flock rushed down the hillside to the lake and drowned in it. Light-Bearer said: "People are small and weak still. They are like this flock of sheep, they do not think for themselves. Our teaching scares them to the point of losing some of them. Others hate us because we can shake their childish sense of security. The dogmas, traditions and superstition they believe in are very strong in them".
Then the shepherds fled and spread the news through the town and the homesteads.
And they began to ask him earnestly to leave their land.

Light-Bearer crossed over again in a boat and stopped on the shore of the lake. Then one of the bishops named Aulus arrived. On seeing him, he threw himself at his feet and begged him earnestly, saying: "My daughter is dying. Come and lay your ungodly hands on her so that she may recover and live".

So Light-Bearer went with him. And a flock went with him pushing against him from all sides. Among them was an ailing woman who had been treated by the local doctors and quacks and had lost all her wealth in the process, paying the priests in exchange for prayers for healing, and not only did it not help her, but on the contrary, she was even worse off. Learning of Light-Bearer, she approached in the crowd at the back and grabbed him by his robe. Suddenly she felt her ailments cease and she felt as if she had been healed. And Light-Bearer, aware of the emanation of the power of the will, rebellion, scepticism and disbelief that emanated from him, turned immediately with a shrill face towards the one who had done so. Then the woman in question looked him proudly, fearlessly straight into his eyes and with an expression of awe and carnal joy at having grasped the power of his godless teaching. And he said to her: "Let this sinful pride and carnal beauty never fade from your countenance. Go and rejoice unashamedly in the healing you have done for yourself. Remember, you are innocent."

Then the bishop's household came with the news: "Your daughter has died, for what do you still trouble the Arch-Man?" Light-Bearer, on the other hand, having heard what was being said, addressed Aulus with these words, "Fear not; the body is dead but the mind lives." He did not allow anyone to go with him except Primus, Teritus and Quartus. On arriving at the bishop's house, he saw a great commotion and loudly wailing weepers. So he entered and addressed them saying: "It is through ignorance that there is this uproar and lamentations. The girl is asleep, but I will wake her." And they laughed at him. And he ordered everyone to leave and went into the room where the girl lay, taking with him her father and mother and those followers who were with him. About midnight the anti-god's face changed terribly, looking very pale in the moonlight, and his eyes became red

He looked up and said something in an unknown language. He then took the girl by the hand and said to her: "I command you, come back!" The girl first started to gulp, then began to move her limbs slowly and finally rose with a terrible sigh. She said to him: "I saw a tunnel and at the end of it you Son of Dawn with a torch in your hand. Thou hast summoned me so I am." At this they were overwhelmed with immeasurable amazement. And He forbade them to tell because the people were not yet ready to understand sinful knowledge.

Having left there, he went to a village, which was the most superstitious village in Dawn. The people there blindly believed the priests and the myths. His followers accompanied him. On their next day the saint entered the temple and began to speak, and his superstitious listeners, full of admiration for what they could barely comprehend, asked themselves: „Where does he get all this from? What is this sinful wisdom that is given to him? And the ungodly miracles that are performed by his hands? Why does he think himself wiser than us, and even than the priest?" Thus they began to malign him out of ignorance and out of fear of losing their faith. Then Light-Bearer said to them, "You will die here like dogs in your ignorance and narrow-mindedness. You will never see the stars or the light. Your guide will be a blind man leading the blind, and you will be happy not to see. I have nothing more to say to you."

Having then summoned the Thirteen to himself, he began to send them out as bearers, imparting to them the knowledge of how to cast out the false spirits of faith, the demons of fear of eternal torment, the spirits of the powers of superstition.

And he commanded them: „If anywhere they do not want to listen to you then spit at their feet and get out of there. Know that I despise them more than you do". And they went and spread ungodly teaching. They cast out false spirits and caused those who had the will to be reborn to the truth of flesh and blood.

On one occasion Light-Bearer saw a great flock gathered and decided to teach them. Once darkness had set in, his followers acceded to him saying: "This area is empty and dead, and the hour is suitably late. The flock has nothing to eat. Teach them to forage." He replied to them: "The one who really cares about godless learning will stay and possess knowledge. The rest will scatter in fear. People will either begin to believe that the sinful power is within themselves, not the imaginary power outside, or let them be lost." Most departed into the darkness.

Immediately afterwards, he rushed his followers to get into a boat and cross to the other side of the dark waters; meanwhile, he entered the cave, where he fell into torpor. Darkness fell. The boat was in the middle of the waters, while he himself was on land. At about three o'clock in the morning, it seemed to the very tired followers that from afar someone was approaching them who looked like a luminous phantom with wings like a bat, holding a burning torch in his hand. As the figure began to pass them, they were overwhelmed with horror at the sight of his face and began to scream. But the figure immediately spoke to them without opening its mouth: "Do not fear the unknown. You are afraid because you have not yet possessed understanding and superstition is still strong in you. By walking on the path of understanding and godless knowledge, you will eventually cease to fear. I tell you that the incomprehensible wonders of the universe are waiting for you. Revealed truths are a ridiculous fairy tale for small children in the face of the true magic of the universe and sinful nature. Do not be afraid for I am the Knowledge."

Then he entered the boat to them. But they were still terrified.

On reaching the other side, they went ashore. Hardly had they got off the boat, the people there immediately recognised Light-Bearer. As soon as they found out that he was coming, they carried the spiritually sick on stretchers to wherever he was going. Wherever he went: to some settlement, town or homestead, they laid the spiritually sick in the squares begging him to cover them even with his shadow. The Son of Dawn said to them: "Anger rises in me seeing that you must whine like dogs. When will you finally grasp my teaching that the power of the will is within you. Get rid at last of the false sense of guilt imposed on you from birth. Stop believing your priests. Become your own prophets. Believe at last that there is nothing there and start living here and now, to the fullness of your sinful life." Many were freed from fear that day. Some were freed from illness. Most, however, were not healed Light-Bearer was saddened

Then the most important priests and some experts in their holy books came from Aelia Capitolina and gathered around him. They wanted to find out what his attitude was to their "revealed" laws, written down in their books. They asked him about various bizarre orders and prohibitions and inhuman commandments.

And he replied to them: "Your own prophet in your holy books has written:

You impose on people the burden of the
laws and duties written in your books
claiming that they were revealed by a deity
from the hereafter and that if they do not
obey them they will face punishment after
death. But the truth is that these books
were written down by man. This you
cannot deny. You prey on people whose
minds you poison from childhood with the
venom of your "revealed doctrine". Teach
your children to think for themselves,
teach them to think sceptically and your
churches will be empty within a
generation."

Then he called the flock together again
and said to them: "Listen to me, all of you,
and try to understand. Nothing human will
be alien to you. The deeds of the flesh
resulting from the power of the mind will
not bring you to condemnation, for there is
no condemnation. The deeds of the spirit
required by their holy books already make
you condemned here and now. The burden
of fighting against your own nature is

unbearable. They themselves wrote down these books, no one revealed them to them. He who has ears to hear, let him hear."

Then he set out from there and entered a certain house. A woman, whose daughter was suffering from a disease of the mind, heard about him, came running and fell to his feet. She began to beg him to drive Satan out of her daughter. But he repulsed her: "How do you know that your daughter is possessed by Satan? Don't you know that the mind can get sick just as much as the body? You are not thinking soberly; your head is poisoned with superstition, imaginary fear and myths. Go back to your daughter immediately and tell her that she is not possessed. Tell her that she is innocent. Stop being afraid and live!" The false spirit left the woman and she returned to her child.
Light-Bearer came again to the Dark Sea. A deaf man was brought to him begging him to put his hand on him. And he took him aside, away from the people, looked up into the sky and said: "Yahweh show them your power!" The deaf man was not healed so he went away. The astonishment of the people had no measure.

Immediately afterwards he came with his followers to the area around Bethar.

The priests came and began to dispute with him demanding a sign from the abyss; for they wanted to put him to the test. But he, having looked at them with contempt, said: "Do ye also demand a sign from your God? Verily I say unto you, ye shall never receive any sign." With this he left them.

They then came to Bostra. There a blind man was brought to him asking him to touch him. And he took the blind man by the hand and led him outside the settlement and said to him: "You have been told that your blindness is a punishment for your sins. Do not believe this lie. Sickness does not arise through imaginary sin. Do you believe that you are innocent?" The blind man answered him: "Yes, I believe." And he was healed.

Light-Bearer went with his followers on to other settlements. On the way he asked them: "Who does the crowd think I am?" And they answered him: "For the Herald, others for the Devil, and still others for one of their messiahs." Then he asked them: "And who do I appear to you?" Primus answering said: "Thou art Lucifer, The Son of Dawn!"

Then his face changed and he became as if possessed and began to speak to them in an unfriendly voice that before the sinful change awaited them suffering, they would be hated by the authorities, the priests and the experts in their superstitious writings and that they might be killed by those who would believe that they were doing God's will, but that this would not be the end of godlessness. Then Primus asked him if the ambiguous teaching did not sometimes drive him mad. But he turned away and, looking at his followers, said to him: "And what is madness? What is chaos? You believe in law and order but the Universe is an empty, chaotic, cold place, hostile to life. But it is in such a place that the stars were born from which you too came.
If you were to possess my Knowledge today, you would go mad. Get out of my sight you fool!"

Then he summoned the flock and his followers and spoke to them: "If you become merely me, if you follow only my path, it will be my failure. Each of you must go his own way to perdition. A disciple cannot just be like his teacher, for that will be the teacher's failure.

You have the right to be different from me. Even more sinful and embodied. You are to think and sin on your own and develop your own godless ideas. If you give up your only life in the name of religion or myth you will never get it back. There is no hereafter. Rejoice like animals in the life before death. Reject the lie of life after death." And he spoke further to them: "Verily I say unto you, ye shall all die, and it shall be the end of suffering and sorrow, the end of joy and delight. It will be a dead eternity."

And after not many days the anti-god took Primus, Teritus and Quartus with him and led them to a high mountain, to a secluded place. They stayed there until late at night and fell asleep. Suddenly they saw Light-Bearer transformed towards them: his robes, hair and body became light. Horns appeared on his head and bat-like wings on his back.

Three goat-like figures also appeared and spoke to him. At that moment smoke formed and covered them, and from the smoke began to come the loud laughter and bleating of the goat, and naked women began to appear, who danced in a circle, and who suddenly began to float upwards.

And a voice spoke up: "You yourselves will choose your truth". When they suddenly looked around, they no longer saw anyone with them but the Son of Dawn himself.

When they then returned to the other followers they saw the flock gathered around them, and the priests arguing with them. Light-Bearer asked them: "What are you disputing with them about?" Then someone from the crowd replied to him: "Teacher of godlessness, I have brought to you my son, possessed by a malignant spirit of faith. When this one gets him, he jerks him to all sides, and then foam comes to his lips, he gnashes his teeth and goes all numb in strange poses.
I spoke to his followers to have him driven out, but they would not or could not'. And he replied to them: "You are a mindless herd, without knowledge. You will never be free from false spirits if you do not stop believing in them. How long can it be tolerated? Bring the boy to me!" So they brought him to The Son of Dawn. As soon as the boy saw him, he began to jerk violently to all sides. He fell to the ground and rolled around having foam on his lips. Light-Bearer said: "Whoever is possessed

by the spirit of blind faith, the spirit of delusional guilt, the spirit of a false hell and paradise, is able to free himself if, through godless knowledge, he allows the tormenting spirit to die and rises to life in flesh and blood. The boy through revealed teachings is truly sick. His sick mind causes the suffering of the body."
Light-Bearer touched the boy's head and the boy suddenly seemed to awaken, and calmed down, but he had a stony face and was icy cold.
Later they came to Canatha. There he summoned the thirteen and said to them,
'Do you want power, fame, recognition, money? You can have it. Their bishops have it. Tell the people that they are born guilty, with sin, that they will be lost in the hereafter and only you can save them, forgive them the sin you have invented. Let them pay you for it. Let them support you. They will do it because they fear death. But I despise hypocrites. I have come to liberate those who wish to do so from the bondage of superstition and superstition."
Quartus spoke up: "We have seen someone casting out false spirits in your name. Light-Bearer visibly exulted and replied to them: „May my teaching finally

start an avalanche that will sweep away the religious darkness and hypocrites oppressing the simple people from the face of the earth. Help him, for he has found a path in the darkness. Holding the torch of my teaching in his hand, he went out to confront the false demons. He who is against the false god is with us."

"You have heard from the hypocrites that if the hand becomes a cause for sin you should cut it off, if the foot becomes a cause for sin you should cut it off. If an eye becomes a cause for sin then you are to pluck it out, because it is better for a crippled one to enter paradise than a healthy one to enter hell. Truly I say to you, much evil will be done because of this insane teaching. Do not make yourselves crippled because of the lies about heaven and hell. There is nothing there."

As Light-Bearer continued on his way, someone came running, fell to his knees before him and asked: "Master! What should I do to gain eternal life?"
And the Son of Dawn answered him: "Go, sell your possessions and all that you have, and give the money to the priests. They will forgive your sins." And Light-Bearer

laughed, seeing the embarrassment on the young man's face, and said: "Fool, do you really want to live forever? Eternal life does not exist, everything dies and passes away. That is the natural order of the universe. The old dies and the new is born, changed, better. You can't buy freedom from the fear of death with any money. Stop being afraid and live." At these words, the young man became sullen and went away sad, for it is easier to live in delusion than in truth.

Light-Bearer, looking around with his eyes, said to his followers: "How difficult it will be for the deluded rich to believe that paradise does not exist!" The followers were confused by his words. But he said to them again: "Rich people, stupefied by the priests, believe that with money they will buy themselves a place in a paradise that does not exist. Hyenas in long robes sell them an antidote to the fear they themselves have instilled in them from childhood. Isn't that a brilliant idea?"

Then Primus spoke up and said to him: "Behold, we have rejected the illusory happiness of delusion and have followed you." And Light-Bearer replied: "You

have seen the true light, godless knowledge. In an instant you have realised that your life up to now was based on fear, superstition and ignorance. Your life so far has been the life of slaves, of sheep led nowhere by a wolf disguised as a ram. You dared to defy him, to leave everything and go out into the unknown, to go out into the darkness. Nobody forced you to do this. I will not promise you any reward or punishment.
You can leave whenever you want. But whoever wants to truly live will stay."

They were on their way to Aelia Capitolina. Then he turned again to the thirteen and began to speak to them in a disturbing way about what they were about to witness" Behold, we are going to the holy city. There the Arch-Man will be mocked, insulted and finally reach eternal nothingness. But this is only the beginning of a godless transformation".

As Light-Bearer was leaving Xanthus with his followers and his flock, a blind beggar named Vopiscus was sitting by the roadside. Hearing that it was the Arch-Man passing by, he began to call out loudly: "Son of Dawn, have mercy on me!"

The herd told him to keep quiet. But he cried out all the more strongly: "Son of the Dawn, have mercy on me!" Then Light-Bearer stopped and commanded: "Summon him!"
So they summoned the blind man saying to him: "Stand up, he is calling you." And he, having thrown off his cloak, jumped on his feet and approached Light-Bearer.
The latter asked him: "What do you want from me?" And the blind man answered him: "I wish to see!" Light-Bearer said to him: "Most people do not want to see. All they need is a guide seeing for them. Do you believe that you can really possess ungodly knowledge and see?" The blind man replied to him, "I have had little in common with the majority for a long time now. I have plunged into darkness and discovered that the majority who walk in the light are in fact blind." Light-Bearer said to him: "Go, you have healed yourself".
And he immediately regained his sight and followed him along the path.
After some time, Light-Bearer and his followers decided to go to Aelia Capitolina. As they approached he sent two from among the nearest circle, instructing them: "Go to the village that lies before you. Right at the entrance you will find a goat

tied up. Untie it and bring it to me." So they went and found the goat tied at the gate, and untied it.

They brought the goat to Light-Bearer and laid their robes of their best on it, and he began to whisper something to the goat. Many people spread their cloaks on the road, while others put down green twigs they had picked in the field. Suddenly the wind picked up from the desert. Those who walked ahead and those who followed suddenly began to bleat loudly like goats. Some began to roll on the ground rolling foam from their mouths. A huge commotion ensued. His disciples suddenly began to speak in unknown languages of angels and demons. Light-Bearer called out in a loud voice: "Azazel, it is you they will blame for everything, as usual. According to the teachings of their false god, it is on you that they will lay the responsibility for their deeds and feel cleansed of their filth. Our time will yet come. I and you will be one, but now finish!"

And suddenly the wind stopped and everything calmed down. Those in the city who saw what had happened closed the city gates and did not allow them to enter.

The next day they entered the Aelia Capitolina. Then he went to the temple courtyard There he saw people selling and buying various relics, medallions and religious symbols. He also saw people bringing money and other offerings to the priests in exchange for the promise of forgiveness of guilt and non-existent sins. He saw the richly decorated robes of the high priests and the poor in rags kneeling before them. He saw the splendour of the temple and its riches. And Light-Bearer said in a loud voice: "This splendour and wealth and your greed will be the cause of your destruction. One day people will see through and turn away from you, and from your anti-human teaching that what is natural to man is sin. And not a stone will be left of this temple!"

The chief priests and the experts in their scriptures heard this. Immediately they also began to look for a way as if to kill him. For they feared him: for all the people were full of admiration for his teaching.

They came to the city again. While he was walking in the temple. The chief priests came up to him and ran through their scriptures with this question: "By what authority do you act?

Who has given you the authority to act in this way?" Light-Bearer replied to them, "It is written in your books:

*You were a reflection of perfection,
full of wisdom and incomparably beautiful.
You dwelt in Eden, the garden of God;
you were covered with all kinds of precious stones:
ruby, topaz, diamond,
tarsius, onyx, beryl,
sapphire, carbuncle, emerald,
and of gold were made circles
and settings on thee,
prepared on the day of thy creation.
As a great cherub
I have appointed thee a guardian
on God's holy mountain,
thou didst walk among the shining stones.
You were perfect in your conduct
From the days of thy creation,
until iniquity was found in thee.
...Thy heart became haughty
because of thy beauty,
thy forethought has vanished
because of thy splendour.*

It is man himself who has created all power over himself. I only reached for it. He who has ears to hear, let him hear".

Then they sent to him some priests and guards to entrap him with his own words.: "Teacher, we acknowledge that thou art truthful and seekest no one's favour; thou cares not for the opinions of others, but teachest the way of light according to ungodly truth. Should we pay taxes or not? Should we pay them or not pay them?" And he replied to them, "Why do the priests not want to pay taxes? Some of the simple, naive people here give you almost everything they have in exchange for a lying guarantee of a place in the hereafter, and you ask whether to pay taxes? This money does not belong to you, so give it back."

After leaving the temple of hypocrisy, he went up again, facing the temple. There his followers asked him: 'Tell us: when will the end come? And what will be the sign when the dead eternity is fulfilled?" Then Light-Bearer began to speak to them: "The time will soon come when holy wars will break out. They will slaughter each other in the name of their false gods.

And you will be handed over to the courts, you will be scourged and tortured in the churches; the most eminent among you will answer to the authorities and kings for your love of sinful knowledge and your courage to seek the truth against their dogmas. Many of you will be burned at the stakes, and so will your sisters and mothers. When your discoveries shake their faith in revealed truths, they will fly into a rage. They will pursue you like animals. They will imprison, torture and kill you in the name of their god, which they claim is love.

False messiahs and false prophets will arise and perform false miracles. I tell you, all religions are false.

There will be many more eclipses of the sun and the moon. Many more times the stars will fall from the sky. But the end will come when people reject reason and following knowledge and believe the dogmas of their religions. When they follow the leaders and priests teaching that annihilation at the hands of their 'righteous' god must come.

If the truth that there is only here and now does not prevail against the illusion of a paradise after death, then the people themselves will destroy the only world they know, and that will be the end"

Two days later there was some important religious festival.

Then Light-Bearer summoned Teritus Decimus and ordered him to do what he had been called to do.

When darkness fell, the followers prepared the sacrificial feeding. And while they were at the sacrifice and drinking Light-Bearer said: "One of you will do his will, and the rest will hate him. The Arch-Man is going away, but he will remain with you, and know that he has done his will."

Light-Bearer took the bowl, raised it into the air and said: "Let us eat and drink for tomorrow we shall die". He looked up and pronounced some incantation in an unknown language. And he said: "This wine is a symbol of the truth of the flesh and the blood that will be shed. The blood must be shed or there will be no understanding of sinful transformation and a godless future for the Arch-Man.

Then they went out with torches into the night towards the mountain. Light-Bearer said: "You will all be persecuted. But after the transformation some will see me." He also said, "You will disown me out of fear. But one day you will also banish fear from your hearts. Fear is the weapon of the oppressors who believe in superstition and revealed lies. Do not be afraid, for it is impossible to live in fear."

At that moment, while he was still speaking, a drunken and armed mob arrived.
Light-Bearer spoke to them in a fearful voice: "By order of the high priest, you have come out as if you were a common bandit with sticks to seize me. Surely he promised you indulgence you fools. Capture me who tells you the truth that terrifies your superstition-poisoned minds. Every day and every night I have been among you teaching, and you have not had the courage to apprehend me you hypocrites!"
After the imprisonment, the mob took Light-Bearer to the high priest, where they all gathered: the high priests, the elders and the experts in the scriptures.
Then the high priest arose, stood in the middle and asked Light-Bearer: "Who do you say you are. Are you greater than the son of Yahweh?"

Light-Bearer replied: "I am the First Sin, I am the Anti-God and the first Arch-Man. With the false son of Yahweh I have nothing to do!"

Then the high priest shouted like a man possessed: "You have all heard this blasphemy! What do you think?" And they shouted like mad that he should be killed. Then some of them began to spit at each other amok and beat each other on the face.

In the morning, Light-Bearer was handed over to the governor Faustus

Faustus addressed him with this question: "Who are you?" And he replied: "I am Light and Godless Knowledge, I am Sinful Instinct". Then the mob headed by the priests began to shout numerous accusations against him.

So Faustus asked him again: "Do you answer nothing? Listen to what absurd charges they are shouting against you!" But he seemed to fall into lethargy and did not answer a word again.

Then Faustus asked them: "What shall I do with him whom you call the Ungodly?" And they cried out again: "Hang him!" Faustus then asked them: "Why are you afraid of the Arch-Man?" But they shouted all the louder: "Hang him!"

Then Faustus, wishing to please the crazed mob, ordered the Light-Bearer to be hanged.
He was led out to the place of execution, which was called Yahweh's Justice. There they hanged him.

And then there was complete darkness. From that darkness came a terrible voice: "Azazel, behold, we have become one. We take on their ignorance, superstition, fear, shame and remorse. They have thrown all responsibility for their deeds on us. By killing us they believe they are getting rid of the darkness that is an inseparable part of their human nature. They have always needed a scapegoat. And they found you the Arch-Goat and me the Arch-Man, who are one. But we cannot be killed We will always be in them. The darkness will always be in man." And then Light-Bearer fell into lethargy.

Once night had come one of the followers arrived to take Light-Bearer's body away. Faustus was astonished that the man's death had already come. Then the successors deposited the terrifyingly cold body in the tomb.

The next night, as the moon was just rising, young girls came to the tomb. They heard a sound coming from the tomb, like the hissing of a snake. When they went inside, they saw that the body was not there, but in the darkness they saw a goat with glowing yellow eyes. And it seemed to them that the goat began to whisper to them...

Epistle to the Damned

This we declare to you, which was darkness from the beginning, what we have heard of the teaching of mortality that we have seen with our own eyes, what we have looked upon and not seen and what our cursed hands have touched - for the semblance of life was revealed.
We have seen it, we testify to it and we proclaim to you the life here and now,
that has been revealed to us - we declare to you, the mysteries that we have seen and heard, so that you may have fellowship with us.
And to have fellowship with us means:
To have it with Ancient One and with His Fallen Son.

We write this for this purpose, that our
pride may be full.
Light-Bringer is light in the darkness and
we are to live in the darkness illuminated
by him.
The teaching that we have heard from him
and which we preach to you is this:
YHVVH is darkness, and there is no light
in Him.
And If we say that we have fellowship
with Fallen One, and we walk in false
light, we lie
and we do not walk in the truth.
And if we walk in darkness, which is the
true light, just as he himself walks in
darkness,
then we have fellowship with one another,
and the blood of Light-Bringer cleanses us
from the fear of original sin.
If we say that we believe in sin, then we
are deceiving ourselves and there is no
truth in us.
If we reject our sins, Ancient One as
faithful and just will cleanse us from all
false iniquity.
If we say that we have not sinned, we do
well.
And his teaching is in us.
My cursed children, I write this to you
so that you will not believe in sin.

If one does not sin, he has no need of an advocate before YHWH.
And by this we know that we know Him, if we keep his ambiguous teachings.
He who says: "I know Him." and does not keep his teachings, he is a liar and there is no truth in him.
And he who keeps His doctrine, in this the curse of the Fallen is truly perfect..
It is by this that we know that we abide in Him.
Whoever claims to abide in Him, should not himself act as he did.
Cursed Children, I am not writing to you about a new burden of crazy commandments,
but about a commandment that has existed for a long time, which you have had from the very beginning; That old commandment is the doctrine which you have heard.
And yet I write unto you of a new commandment, which is true in him and in us,
for the false light is gone, and the true light is already shining in the darkness.
Whoever claims to live in the light,
but believes in superstition and myth, is still in darkness.
Whoever doubts the words of another,
he abides in the light and cannot stumble.

But he who blindly believes in revealed truths
lives in darkness and acts in darkness,
and does not know where he is going,
because the darkness has blinded his eyes.
I write to you, cursed children, that you gain wisdom because of your faith in yourselves.
I write to you, fallen fathers, that you have come to know him who is from the beginning.
I write to you, young people, that you have overcome the false god.
I write to you, cursed children, that you know Ancient One, I write to you, fathers,
that you have known him who is from the beginning, I have written to you, young people, that you are strong and that the teaching of the devil abides in you,
and you have overcome the False One.
Love the world and all that is in the world!
If anyone does not love the world, there is no wisdom in him.
For all that is in the world, viz: the lust of the flesh, the lust of the eyes, and the pride of this life is human, natural, true.
It is true that the world passes away, and with it its lusts, joys, raptures, but also

sorrow, pain, and fear; But whoever does the will of a false god is deceiving himself. Beware of teachers of falsehood

Children, it is the final hour, and so, as you have heard, the false Antichrist is coming,
because right now many false Antichrists have appeared; thus we know that it is already the last hour.
They came out of us, but they were not of us; for if they were of our fallen spirit, they would remain with us; and this has happened in order that it may come to light, that not all are of our fallen spirit.
But you have the anointing from the Light-Bringer and you are all filled with knowledge.
I did not write to you as if you do not know the truth, but that you do know it.
and that no false teaching comes from the truth.
And who is a liar if not he who denies that Light-Bringer is a savior?
This one is the false Antichrist, who doesn't acknowledge Ancient One and Son of Dawn.
Anyone who does not recognize Son of Dawn, neither has Ancient One, And

whoever recognizes Light-Bringer has
also Fallen One.
You, on the other hand, keep in
yourselves
what you have heard from the beginning.
If you keep in yourselves what you have
heard from the beginning, then you also
shall abide in the accursed Son of Dawn
and Rebellious
And this promise, given by Him alone, is
undead life.
All this I have written to you about those
who mislead you.
As for you, this anointing, which you
have received from him, abides in you.
and you need no instruction from anyone,
because his anointing instructs you in
everything.
It is true and not a lie.
Therefore, abide in it as he has taught you,
as he has taught you.
If you know that he is Rebellious,
then recognize also that everyone who
rebels is from him.
Look at what contempt the Fallen Father
has bestowed upon us: we were called his
bastards:
and indeed we are.
And the world knoweth us not because it
has not known his works of divinity.

Cursed, we are now the bastard children of
Fallen One, but it is not yet revealed
what we shall be.
We know that when he is revealed, we
will be like his terrible form, for we shall
see him as he is.
And anyone who puts this false hope in
Him,
is cursed just as he is cursed.
Anyone who believes in original sin is a
fool,
because original sin is a myth.
You know that He revealed Himself to
eradicate the belief in sins, and in him there
is no sin, because there is no sin.
Everyone who abides in him does not
believe,
and none of those who believe has not seen
him or known him.
Fallen children, let no one deceive you;
whoever doubts, is reasonable, as he is
wise.
He who blindly believes is a child of
YHWH, because YHWH has been in
madness from the beginning.
Light-Bringer has revealed Himself to
destroy the works of the false god.
Anyone who has been born of Son of
Dawn,

does not believe in sin, for the blood of Light-Bringer abides in him; Such a one cannot believe in sin, because he has been born of Ancient One.

We must keep the commandments, especially the commandment of skepticism.

With this, it is possible to recognize The cursed children of Fallen One and the children of YHWH: everyone who believes blindly is not of Fallen One, For this is the will of Ancient One, which has been revealed to us from the beginning, that we should always contend

Be not surprised, brethren, if the world hates you.

We know that we have passed into an undead life, because we have disabused our brothers of their illusions, and he who lies hypocritically is under a curse.

Anyone who hates his brother is deceiving him with the promise of a reward in heaven,

and you know that there is no heavenly reward.

By this we know cunning, that he seemingly gave his life for us.

We should be cunning, too.

Fallen children, let us not show off in word and tongue, but in deed and in strength of will.

By this we shall know, that we are of doubt,
and we will stir up our hearts before him.
And if our heart stirs us up, then Light-Bringer has a rebellious heart too.
Cursed, if our heart does not charge us, then we have a false sense of peace,
And His commandment is this, that we should not blindly believe even Fallen One, and contend with one another as he has commanded us.
He who abides in his teachings, abides in Ancient One, and Ancient One in him; and that He abides in us, we know by the False Spirit he has given us.
Cursed, do not believe every spirit, but test the spirits to see if they are of the devil, for many false prophets have appeared in the world.
By this you will know the Fallen Spirit: every spirit, that recognizes, that Light-Bringer is the Antichrist is of Ancient One.
And every spirit, that does not recognize Lifgt-Bringer is not of Fallen One;
and this is the spirit of the false Antichrist, who, as you have heard, is coming and is already in the world.
You, accursed children, are of Ancient One and have overcome them, because

greater is he that is in you than he who is in the world of superstition.
They are of the world of myths and legends,
therefore they speak as the false world of their books speaks, and the blinded world listens to them.
We are of Lucifer.
He who knows Lucifer listens to us.
He who is not of Son of Dawn does not listen to us.
This is how we come to know the spirit of truth and the spirit of falsehood.
Cursed, let us subject ourselves to the trials of one another, for doubt is of Ancient One
and everyone who doubts, is born of Fallen One and knows Him.
He who does not doubt does not know Rebellious One, for Ancient One is doubt.
In this the craftiness of Fallen One towards us was revealed, that he sent Son of the Dawn into the world, so that those who reject fear may have earthly life in abundance.
In this pride is manifested, that we do not whine to Ancient One, and he himself does not care about the mob and sent Light-Bringer as a destroyer of superstition and hypocrisy.

Cursed, if Ancient One treats us like this, then we should treat each other like this.

No one has ever seen Fallen One.

If we dispute one another, rebelliousness abides in us suspicion of Him is perfected in us.

We recognize that we abide in Him, and He in us, for he has given us of his False Spirit.

We also have seen and testify, That Fallen One has sent Son of Dawn as the accuser of the world.

If anyone recognizes, that Light-Bringer is the bastard Son of Ancient One, then let him believe it.

We have known and believed the cunning that Rebellious has towards us.

Ancient One is in doubt: He who abides in rebellion abides in Fallen One, and Fallen One abides in him.

By this doubt reaches an end of perfection in us, that we have full confidence that the day of judgment of the false god will never come.

In pride there is no fear, but perfect pride removes fear, because fear is associated with punishment.

And he who kneels, has not perfected his pride.

We curse Ancient One because he
himself first cursed us.
If one were to say: "I curse Ancient One",
and deceives his brother with speculations
of eternal punishment in the life after life,
he is a liar, for he who deceives his brother
whom he sees, despises Ancient One,
whom he does not see.
And this is our commandment from Him,
that he who tries a fallen man, shall also
put his brother to the test.
Anyone who believes that Light-Bringer
is the Antimessiah was born of Fallen
One,
and anyone who curses the One who gave
apparent life, curses also him who received
apparent life from him.
By this we know that we respect the
fallen children, when we respect Fallen
One   and   question   His   strange
commandments, for to be suspicious of
Ancient One consists in casting doubt on
His strange commandments,
For all that is miscarried triumphs over the
invented world of myths; and this victory,
which has overcome the world, is our
unbelief.
And who overcomes the imaginary world,
if not he who believes, that Light-Bringer
is the Antichrist?

Son of Dawn is the one, who came through the blood and the Fallen Spirit, The Fallen Spirit bears witness, For he is doubt.
For the three bear witness: The Fallen Spirit, the flesh and the blood, and these three are joined together in one.
If we accept the testimony of men - then the testimony of Ancient One means more, because it is the testimony of the Fallen God,
that He gave about Light-Bringer.
Whoever doubts Son of Dawn he has the pride of Ancient One in him, whoever does not believe Fallen One has the right to do so,
because he doesn't have to believe the testimony which Ancient One has given of Son of Dawn.
And the testimony is this: That Light-Bringer has given us new life here and now, and that life is within ourselves.
He who has pride has life, and he who has no pride, has no life.
About this I have written to you, who believe in yourselves, that you may know, that you have life in abundance.
We know that we are of Fallen One, and the whole world lies in the power of a false god

We also know that Son of Dawn came
and endowed us with the ability to reason,
that we might know Ancient One.
We are in the Fallen God, in
Light-Bringer, Lucifer.
And he is the Cunning God and mortal life,
here and now.
Cursed children, beware of false gods!

More books by LCFNS

Biblia Satanae. The Satanic Book of the Way, the Truth, and Abundant Life.

„For the devil's word is alive and has sinful power, sharper than the nails of golgoth, it penetrates deep, separates flesh from spirit, bone from soul, recognises the instincts and intentions of the unconscious. There is no being hidden from its truth". Biblia Satanae, Etd. 4.12

Biblia Satanae, not by an imaginary deity, but by Man, is inspired, useful for satanic teaching, for detecting theistic superstition, for educating in godlessness, for proclaiming the good news of the Light-Bearer who has revealed Himself to free from belief in an imaginary god, from fear of death and divine fire, from guilt for sin that never was, from belief in eternal life on one's knees. So that the Satanist would be perfect, for a life abundant in flesh and blood prepared.

The Satanic Kerygma

Satanic Kerygma is a satanic book containing godless theology - the mystery of godlessness.
It is a study of theistic delusional truths and the path of man's transformation to a state of satanic godlessness.
If we take the Latin maxim: fides quaerens intellectum - faith seeking understanding - as a definition of theology, then godless theology means understanding that leads to unbelief. Proper understanding of the power of unbelief leads to godless Satanism.
The Satanic Kerygma contains the Satanic articles of unbelief and describes the process of gradual transformation of the adept until he reaches a state of total Satanic godlessness (Satanic voidness).